EXCHAN

Editor Jude Brigley

EXCHANGES
POEMS BY WOMEN IN WALES

Honno Poetry

Published by Honno
'Ailsa Craig'   Heol y Cawl   Dinas Powys
South Glamorgan   CF6 4AH

First impression 1990
© *Jude Brigley, introduction*
© *The Poets*

British Library Cataloguing in Publication Data

Exchanges: a collection of poems by women in Wales.
I. Brigley, Jude
821.9140809287

ISBN 1-870206-08-8

Published with the financial support of the Welsh Arts Council

Cover illustration by Barbara Crow
Designed by Ruth Dineen

Typeset in Garamond by Megaron, Cardiff
Printed by Gwasg John Penry, Swansea

ACKNOWLEDGEMENTS

The publishers gratefully acknowledge the permission of the following: *Anglo-Welsh Review* for 'Chutney Jars' (vol. 78, 1985) by Sue Moules, 'The Bronchoscopy Session' and 'The Villages' (vol. 76, 1984) by Madeline Mayne; Carcanet for 'A Saturday in the '20s' from *Trial of Strength* by Jean Earle, and for 'Miracle on St David's Day', 'Swinging', 'Heron at Port Talbot', 'Last Rites', 'Missa Pontcanna' from Gillian Clarke's *Selected Poems*, and for 'Neighbours' from Gillian Clarke's *Letting in the Rumour*; Poetry Wales Press for 'English Lesson' and 'Exchange' from Christine Evans's *Looking Inland*; *Poetry Wales* for 'Name' (vol.19, 1983); Seren Books for 'Out of the Shadows', 'Conversation 1', 'Father goes blackberrying' and 'Thinking about Harry' from Eleanor Cooke's *A Kind of Memory*, and 'Riding it Out' from Christine Evans's *Cometary Phases*.

CONTENTS

PREFACE

The son of a famous poet was on his way to a poetry reading to hear his parent read. As he entered the hall, someone took him aside and told him that his father had sadly died after fighting a debilitating illness for some years. In a state of shock, he stumbled into the hall and took his seat. As he glanced at the lectern his mother came forward and started to read a poem. Can you account for this? Perhaps you have heard the story before and you are feeling quite superior in seeing through my ploy. A class of fourteen year olds assumed that the father was the poet and that the mother was simply filling in. Like all riddles it is obvious once you have seen it, but it serves to illustrate the sort of assumptions which may lie deep in our consciousness.

Women writers have often been treated with an attitude which smacks of astonishment – not so much that it is done well but that it is done at all. This book is a celebration of what women writers have achieved in Wales. It will be enjoyed by both the casual reader and the student of English literature. It is not a special favour to women writers. It is simply that modern examinations deliver poetry into the hands of pupils and teachers and with this new freedom we can redress the balance so that no school child can look back as Gloria Evans Davies has and say:

> There were no books by women in the schools I went to. If a token woman writer had crossed my childhood path, even if only to come in praise of men, the image of her alone as a woman writer would have given me a 'room of my own'. (*Poetry Wales*, 23(1),37)

As a teacher I sympathize with Penny Windsor when she said: 'I was once a teacher and taught "Ten Contemporary Poets" at O level. They were all men.'

I do not know if there is any substantial difference between the poetry of men and women. It is obvious that male writers can write about female experiences with insight and even feminist sympathy. I would never decry the power of the imagination and our astonishing human capacity to enter like Keats the pecking bird outside his window. Yet, women writers themselves are divided as to whether there is a difference between a man's mind and a woman's. Katherine Ann Porter has asserted, 'I'm sure there is', while Sheenagh Pugh who feels so strongly on the issue that she is not included in this volume has written, 'I do not believe that minds have genders.' What many women writers agree on is that writing by women should not be treated as a special category. Margaret Atwood has tried to get around this by coining the category WWAAV (Writers Who Are Also Women).

My own feeling is that to be born a woman is to be encouraged to develop certain aspects of the personality. I would agree with Robert Frost when he said that a poet cannot write the poetry he wants to write but only the poetry that is in him. And her. That does not mean that I think that poetry written by women is inferior. I think that the experiences of women enrich and open out the subject-matter of poetry. In order to argue with this proposition the reader will have to examine the poems in detail, for this is an anthology to be thought about as well as celebrated and enjoyed.

The story of the poet's son illustrates the need for role models which are occasionally local and include our sexual group. It is not that poetry by women is for women, men for men, West Indians for West Indians. In introducing young people to poetry there must be variety, breadth and many openings in the fence. This book works on the premiss that a good starting-point is the local, the alive and, in this case, female writers. However, any anthology is but a stone thrown in the sea to make further ripples and connections elsewhere.

Jude Brigley

Publishers' note
Teachers' notes are available from Honno, 'Ailsa Craig', Heol y Cawl, Dinas Powys, South Glamorgan. Please send an A4 addressed envelope and stamps to the value of 75p.

WORDS

How long does it take you to write a poem

It has taken me

    5 years

      3 months

        and 1 day

to write this poem

22 daydreams
31 false starts
13 and a $\frac{1}{2}$ bottles of home-made wine
10 farts
10 hiccups
64 sneezes
3 long distance phone calls
a day trip to Barry
91 trips to 'The Tenby'
50 casual conversations
a daily and expensive counselling session
extensive visits to the British Museum
5 notebooks, 6 biros and a perm

and 43 assaults on people who ask
how long does it take you to write a poem.

Penny Windsor

Words

I have words in my head
Like fish
Swimming round and round
Their oval world.
But only some manage to
Reach the island,
And even fewer are
Strong enough to
Strip the fleshy fruit
From the husky tree.

Sarah Francis

The Woman Poet

stumbles up from a disjointed sleep
to children's voices. The room is dark,
rain dulls the hidden window.
A dream, vibrant
hangs round her:
she eases it like a shawl
away and it fades
as she gropes for slippers.

Behind the breakfast clatter she finds tears
rising and falling, and anger
comes and goes. Outside
there are trees vivid with moss in the wet wind
and leaves falling, and rubbery bright
fungi sparking the gloom.
Perhaps tomorrow
there will be time. The trees blow words at her
as she gathers plates
and her mind lifts and clears.

Poems spill out of the tips
of her fingers and slide around
in the dishwater suds;
are slipped down the sink
where they spiral
and eddy for just
a moment. Then down
that black hole with a rude suck
and a derisive gurgle
they go. She smiles:
her lips are sealed.

Hilary Llewellyn-Williams

Miracle on St David's Day

'They flash upon that inward eye
Which is the bliss of solitude'

(*The Daffodils* by William Wordsworth)

An afternoon yellow and open-mouthed
with daffodils. The sun treads the path
among cedars and enormous oaks.
It might be a country house, guests strolling,
the rumps of gardeners between nursery shrubs.

I am reading poetry to the insane.
An old woman, interrupting, offers
as many buckets of coal as I need.
A beautiful, chestnut-haired boy listens
entirely absorbed. A schizophrenic

on a good day, they tell me later.
In a cage of first March sun a woman
sits not listening, not seeing, not feeling.
In her neat clothes the woman is absent.
A big, mild man is tenderly led

to his chair. He has never spoken.
His labourer's hands on his knees, he rocks
gently to the rhythms of the poems.
I read to their presences, absences,
to the big, dumb labouring man as he rocks.

He is suddenly standing, silently,
huge and mild, but I feel afraid. Like slow
movement of spring water or the first bird
of the year in the breaking darkness,
the labourer's voice recites 'The Daffodils'.

The nurses are frozen, alert; the patients
seem to listen. He is hoarse but word-perfect.
Outside the daffodils are still as wax,
a thousand, ten thousand, their syllables
unspoken, their creams and yellows still.

Forty years ago, in a Valleys school,
the class recited poetry by rote.
Since the dumbness of misery fell
he has remembered there was a music
of speech and that once he had something to say.

When he's done, before the applause, we observe
the flowers' silence. A thrush sings
and the daffodils are flame.

Gillian Clarke

Case History

There was a boy of twelve who'd never learned
To speak. Farm-bred, he had not understood
That he was more than livestock – turned
To dogs for company, came running for his food
With cats or chickens and woke with no surprise
At owls' homecoming or starbreath on his face.
I saw him when they brought him in. His eyes
Were clear as sunlit water, held a space
We promptly crammed with language. Beyond reach
Soft wordless songs, the colours in wet stone
He loved; grass-smell; the old humanity of touch.
His brightness died and we began to realize
Speech wakes in us so confident, so soon,
What deeper dumbnesses might it disguise?

Christine Evans

SWINGING

The Gardener's Daughter

In the gloom of a dusty shed
  lay seed potatoes, ranks of knobble faces
staring at me, exhaling a sharp reek
  of the underworld, stopping my breath with mould.
I'd sit with them, half-afraid,
  listening to the tinny noise of rain
and your voice from the outer world of the stone yard.

Your movements were large and slow
  steady, skilful, lifting a laden barrow
with ease, in the long light of the afternoon,
  or in the sea-light of the glasshouses
you strung tomato trusses
  with their heavy, jungle smell,
and played the monsoon of the snaking hose.

My movements were quick and small
  making my feet ring on the iron floor
following you along the leafy rows
  plucking out weeds to please you.
Squat in my rubber boots I'd fill the pots
  shovelling compost with my narrow trowel
proudly wearing my work in my fingernails.

I held the slipping knots
  as we wound raffia round squeaking stems
of tulips, freesias, dahlias: but you
  carried the precious flowers in your huge hands
much gentler than mine, to the water.
  And I, the gardener's daughter,
my face in the swimming blooms, conjuring rainbows.

Hilary Llewellyn-Williams

Swinging

At the end of the hot day it rains
Softly, stirring the smells from the raked
Soil. In her sundress and shorts she rocks
On the swing, watching the rain run down
Her brown arms, hands folded warm between
Small thighs, watching her white daps darken
And soak in the cut and sodden grass.

She used to fling her anguish into
My arms, staining my solitude with
Her salt and grimy griefs. Older now
She runs, her violence prevailing
Against silence and the avenue's
Complacency, I her hatred's object.

Her dress, the washed green of deck chairs, sun
Bleached and chalk-sea rinsed, colours the drops,
And her hair a flag, half and then full
Mast in the apple-trees, flies in the face
Of the rain. Raised now her hands grip tight
The iron rods, her legs thrusting the tide
Of rain aside until, parallel
With the sky, she triumphs and gently
Falls. A green kite. I wind in the string.

Gillian Clarke

Riding it out

Wind and rain
made an ocean of the air
the day you chose to be born
Angharad. Sea gulped
at the grey land. No coming ashore
could be easy – and you
supposed to turn
to dive headfirst into the light
to be held up and recognized –
you just waited, jammed in tight, the wrong
way round.

But it was even more miraculous
the way they folded back
muscle and skin like fanned-out petals
to make an opening
to lift you, glistening, out

your eyes already open, steady,
as if you'd always known
it was the only way
to break your mooring-rope to darkness
the pulsing birthcord
wound tightly, twice
round the stem of your neck.

Christine Evans

Steps

The first step was visiting.
He brought flowers.
They would dine,
Play music, laugh late.
Then, one morning,
He was still there.

The big step was the marriage.
A pagan bridesmaid,
I romped anxiously,
Threw confetti, pricked
My fingers on her roses,
Wished my dad were there.

Living together, I was
Always out of step,
The unequal angle
In a two-sided triangle.
On walks she gave her hand
To me, but gave her mind to him.

At night time now,
Upon the stairs,
I shut my eyes and shrink.
When little, I scaled
This mountain range and
She redeemed my night.

Gillian Fothergill

Taking Root

The field is bare now, spiked
Only by sprays of lush grass, clods
Weighting my boot with their dough
Uneveness. I trace the sinking
Footprints to each brim of field,
Restoring to memory the curves and
Undulations, the gaps through hedges, the big
Trees, the electric towers stretching
Their wires over the fat horizon.
Not much has changed except
The season – a bramble mesh netting

Old pathways. Wheat once measured
My height here. It came up to my chin.
You had to run and swim with arms
To split a parting through its thickness.
In the middle of this square
Was where I lay, flattening a space;
Walls of wheat; floors of crumpled straw –
All itching and crackling. Blue sky
Made the pods seem riper, ready
To pop. I peeled their husks, layer
By layer, reaching the white core, biting
Off their tops. Then spitting them high
Into the air – and everything was
There – a whole world contained. Over

The next hill, the fields were stored,
Their bud-greens deepening. And now
Each hill is bald – colours are sepia,
Scumbled earth. Yet somehow purer,
Each tone delicate in its difference.
My eye recedes from faint distances,
Shapes of trees, moving across clods
As they ripple nearer. Close my eyes,
And in the mud of memory, wheat is growing,
Blocking all vision, sprouting more yellow,
Richer than it ever did before.

Frances Williams

When Mam Comes Home

When mam comes home
she will be like some other mother
in her slippery bright dress and tripping heels.
A newsreader mouth.
Her hair will smell of old talk.

She will come in quietly
as if sorry for the draught.
Mac will jump and wag to meet her.
She will bend over the tomato plants
to say how they have grown.

When mam comes home
I will tell her dad and I had fun
breaking eggs and frying bacon.
She will reach across to us
with questions, but glance away.
Leave us stranded with the answers.

She will talk to us too loud
and her hands will jump about
as if they needed stroking.
I will sit close, wishing I could sniff her clothes
to read where she has been, what new film
has been set running in her head.

When mam comes home
I will wait for her to notice my pyjamas folded
and my tidy bed. But I will not let
her arm go round me
until she sags into her own shape
forgets to brush her hair
until her colours get turned down
and she smells of us again.

Perhaps she will be home by morning.

Christine Evans

EXCHANGE

Exchange

I am doing The Red Pony
With 3B. Despite their appetite
For murder, horror films
And modern cannibals, they
Are easily moved
By animals. Aloud, they wonder
About the first that shared our lives:
Dogs, they agree, and orphaned goats,
Suggests the girl whose mother keeps
The wholefood shop. But '*Cows*, Miss?'
They do not see have anything,
Save meat and milk, to give.
So I do not try to tell them

How with the first cow that we bought,
Old, scarred and belly-sagged
With breeding, for a time I found
An old affinity, a new
Exchange. She had rosettes like flowers
Hidden in her glossy hide;
Her throat was soft as catkins
In the sun. She stood
Hock-deep in meadowsweet
Sighing as I milked her;
On winter mornings, breathed its fragrance
Through the stone cowshed. I warmed my hands
On her blackness, my heart with her trust.

It was February, before dawn, hard frost
Squeezing the land to silence
When we loaded her. The concrete
Glistened like black slate.
It took my voice,

My hand on her flank, to get her
Stumbling up the ramp.
'Well done, Missus!' And I stood back
Smiling, as the bolts went home.
Eighty pence per kilo
On the hook. She was barren.
Useless. But I am glad
It was too dark to see her eyes.

Christine Evans

The English Master

We passed through his grey eye
Like conscripts. We, those before us,
Those to come. Faceless.

Dully engaged in battle,
He took moods
To man the guns alone,
Passionate in smoke.
Outposts of words
(Beyond the planned attack)
Went up in flames.
Such assaults gained few prisoners . . .
Upward, uneasy glances.
He had known historical war
In defence of us –
Faceless past, present and not-yet-here,
His poor country, dumb native land.
A silver plate in his head
Gave occasional trouble,
Then he'd retreat
Behind the desk.

'Get on with your work!'

He would lend a book
Into a startled hand. 'Keep it clean – '
As a jaded tourist
Drops his ritual coin
Into the fountain.

Jean Earle

English Lesson

They strip the centuries from me
With their eyes, these hostile women
And the boys in the desks at the back
Hunching over their sullenness
Whenever I look their way.
So, helpfulness becomes
A patronage. We are doing précis
From past papers. Not my idea,
The syllabus, I tell them, I cannot help
The system; but feel only
That I strut and harangue
Them, captive as if
Their names and liveries
Were owed to me, their passage
Still unpaid. And when one boy
Sighing, too hot, rubs at his neck,
I seem to see the chains
As if an enforced march
Through forest still continues;
And temper bares
A ruthless Saxon bitch
Lashing them with their ineptitude.
Backed up against the blackboard I recall
It's fear
That makes the she-wolf snarl.

Christine Evans

Lunchtime Lecture

And this from the second or third millenium
B.C., a female, aged about twenty-two.
A white, fine skull, full up with darkness
As a shell with sea, drowned in the centuries.
Small, perfect. The cranium would fit the palm
Of a man's hand. Some plague or violence
Destroyed her, and her whiteness lay safe in a shroud
Of silence, undisturbed, unrained on, dark
For four thousand years. Till a tractor in summer
Biting its way through the long cairn for supplies
Of stone, broke open the grave and let a crowd of light
Stare in at her, and she stared quietly back.

As I look at her I feel none of the shock
The farmer felt as, unprepared, he found her.
Here in the Museum, like death in hospital,
Reasons are given, labels, causes, catalogues.
The smell of death is done. Left, only her bone
Purity, the light and shade beauty that her man
Was denied sight of, the perfect edge of the place
Where the pieces join, with no mistakes, like boundaries.

She's a tree in winter, stripped white on a black sky,
Leafless formality, brow, bough in fine relief.
I, at some season, illustrate the tree
Fleshed, with woman's hair and colours and the rustling
Blood, the troubled mind that she has overthrown.
We stare at each other, dark into sightless
Dark, seeing only ourselves in the black pools
Gulping the risen sea that booms in the shell.

Gillian Clarke

Advice on Pregnancy

What is pregnancy?
It's obviously an issue to be treated seriously
involving, as it does, the future of the human race.
The Magic of Pregnancy is much talked about
by men and superwomen
but here I offer a little practical advice
for the woman in the street.

First you will need the ability
to pee into a small bottle
accurately, before breakfast, and stop midstream
(remember to wash the bottle first or
expect a health visitor
relentlessly pursuing contaminated samples).

Secondly, an affinity with plastic dolls helps.
There are lots of these in the ante-natal clinic
all wearing nappies in different styles.

Thirdly, acquire a thorough knowledge
of all the public loos —
exact location, cost and comfort.

Next, an ability to move bulk.
Placing a demi-john on a shelf
is good practice for travelling on a bus
Also try driving an overloaded lorry with care.

Fifth — Association.
Only associate with thin women
More than one pregnant/overweight woman
seen together
is a joke.

And sixth, don't let it show
or let it all show.
In pregnancy there is no middle way
a Bump is a Bump.

Seventh, don't worry about 'internals'
men are experienced at this kind of thing.

Lastly, *Learn the Signs*.
Chelsea buns and chips are not a normal meal
Five minute labour pains are not a) diarrhoea b) belated
    period pains c) cramp d) psychosomatic
Ignore advice that it's natural and doesn't hurt
also stories of African women and bushes –
these are the fantasies of male academics.
Note that the majority of husbands who faint during labour
    like large families
and that hospitals that want you to come again have a vested
    interest – ignore them.

and any advice to forget the pain, the inconvenience, the
    humiliation
WRITE IT DOWN

these are just some practical points to remember
about pregnancy and its magic.

Penny Windsor

DIS-
-LOCATION

Dis-

I love my love con amore, because he is.

I love my love with my   being,
                    confidently,
                    doubly because he loves,
          with eagerness and
                    fear,
                    gauchely
        I love him.
    I love my love – I –
             my joyous
                    kindly
                    love
  because he is magic . . . .

Come, come! This is a private poem. What is the difference between magic and . . . . doesn't matter.

What is the difference between contrivance and poetry?

A poem

There was a fire –
Let us take this thought –
That yearned to consume one particular, much desired –
Shall we call it a leaf? –

                    that was always just out of reach.
When eventually the leaf fell into the fire it found only cold grey ash.
(Would Schubert have liked this thought?)
The same wind that blew away the leaf fanned the fire into flame again.

Dear God, Dearest God,

I have been examining basic philosophies –
Whether what is is or is not –
Will it be? and if so, will it or not.

Two love limericks

This isn't the usual form
For describing emotional storm –
But then, who can tell?
If it can be done well
It may become one day the norm.

My God, the whole sky is ablaze!
I expect it is only a phase
That will certainly pass
As it always has
When it's happened on previous days.

A story

There was a butterfly woken too soon from its winter.

He flew to me and clung, his feet light, a vibration only. There was a
need of me.
I will succour him.

He asked for ? something – and I brought him sweet.
I brought him sugar in a gilded dish.
What a butterfly! Eyes he has and sees not.

Dearest Father, this is all I ask, that you hold him tenderly, tenderly, in the hollow of your hand.

He is waiting somewhere. Is there fear? My peacock has gone,
So I am alone – but the butterfly is dying.

Will they make a film of my poem, or is it the part that is always left out?
The ending has been changed, The first, in words, I thought I understood, has been lost – thrown into some fire perhaps.

Hopes Springs, Inferno. That is my address.
'Drop Thy still dews.' Dona nobis pacem.
Hold your peace.
Hold – hold – hold.
Non confundar in aeternam.

I love my love with an x because he is unknown,
                    is the question why
                    is omega, is at an end,
                    a ghost that will not lie down.
Libera me.

-location

Madeline Mayne

The Song of Blodeuwedd on May Morning

Skilful woman am I
and dancing woman am I
turning and turning on the green
skin of the dawn fields:
woman of light am I, my morning eyes
too clear, too bright for you.

With calmness, with care,
with breast milk, with dew,
my web I weave
my spell I cast on you.

With calmness, a still point
that the world spins around
I am pulled up out of the ground
my spell has found you.

Beauty above and below me,
beauty behind and before me,
beauty surrounds me
and I sound, I resound like a drum.
I am making my magic, my power;
flying woman who soars to the sun
am I, lovely Goddess woman
covered in rainbows, in feathers, in flowers.
Dark my mind with visions of stars
of the night I have seen, where I have been;
See! I have chosen you.

Strong young man, a man of trees
of river-shadows, of hills, of horns;
all new and secret, my moon-mate,
I await you on the cold breeze
that brings you to me stumbling warm
from your bed, oh yes, with care,
with milk and with dew
I draw you to me on my white thread.
When you hear my voice, my cry
when you see the oak blossoming
when you feel the owls pass by
fetch your staff and run from your door –
it is I, woman of flowers, who calls
who holds wide her wings for you.
With beauty behind, with beauty before;
with calmness, with care,
with breastmilk, with dew
this stone I place: I bathe my face
and I wait for you.

Hilary Llewellyn-Williams

Pebbles

You bend down.
It irritates me.
I hate people who pretend interest:
It's just a show.
A pebble, I state;
My sarcasm shows.
Oh no it's not just a pebble.
Your reply is of the expected.
You make wonderful things of pebbles,
Using your imagination of course,
You were never the craftsman.

That's where we differ.
You think: I know.
We argue: you walk off.
I sit on the pebbles.
Only the sea is important to me.

Kate Cumming

Lovespoon

He carves
    A lovespoon,
In the cool
    Of the dairy trees,
For one
    He does not love
With his true love in mind
        Who gathers rushes
For a rush light
      On the mountains
    His unbeloved owns,
And wears and hugs
      The silver furs
    Of the silver pools.
In the autumn
    He shapes
      The cherrywood
On his knee
    Steadier
Than the rickety
      Kitchen table
Pausing only
    When his mother
Takes the oil lamp
    To the pantry
Leaving him
    In a firelight glow.
        Decayed petals
Sleep,
    Winter birds
      Hanging in the wind
    As if on game hooks
      In his pantry;

He rides in splendour
   With his bride
  Over the hills
Of his forsaken love's
    Footprints,

And deep
 In the glittering nights
His unloved one
   Breathes as gently
As the lovespoon,
    The spring snow

  Giving way
To hedge-hopping
    Violets.

Gloria Evans Davies

The Woman who Knits

The woman who knits
is dangerous

he didn't realise that

he understood the obvious motion of needles
clacking into some kind of eternity
the intensity of fingers
dedicated to secret and intricate patterns
combined with the blank look at the telly

he recognised the refusal to communicate
in anything but platitudes

he knew some of the signs

for instance, he knew the tendency
to start counting
when a difficult question arose
the changing of colours suddenly
at the punch line of his latest joke
muttering like some witches' chant
deep pink to scarlet red, dark blue to indigo

and half way up the sleeve
he knew a family row would bring a shout
'Knit, pearl and tbl
yarn forward, two together
loop, decrease
and cast off three
on each alternate row'

that night he stayed out too late
and came in drunk
the stitches tightened
the tension changed
he thought she was
just knitting

and when
as was his usual way
he turned his back
he did not hear her yell
'join arm and neckband seams
cast off; don't press'

and next day
the jumper made
she'd gone

Penny Windsor

Name

On marriage she changed her name,
tried to become a part of his heritage
but failed,
losing her self-confidence
her warmth of being her.
At the divorce
she lost half of everything
which had defined her personality:
the house, car, ornamental plants.
Was left with the children
stamped with his name,
looking out of eyes
that belonged with him.
Even her name was alien;
she felt a fraud
too advanced to salvage
pieces of her former self.

Sue Moules

Perhaps I'm Normal Too

I didn't know another woman looked like me
I didn't know I wasn't a freak

I longed to be slim and neat
with stand-up breasts
and skin-tight jeans
on a small but cheeky bum
I longed for mini-skirt thighs
I longed to be petite or statuesque
I longed to be other than me

So when we swam together at Pwll Du
the sea entirely ours
I was surprised
to see you
broad and floppy, wide and sexy, plump and messy
just like me

I didn't know another woman looked that way
Perhaps your normal woman looks that way
Perhaps I'm normal too.

Penny Windsor

Snake-dance

You come hesitant to my door,
weighed down with case
and a hard clean stone of grief.
Five years, and the small death
of our friendship comes to life
like the sun in your hair,
the touch of cold hands in my fingers.
Your tears are slow, reminding me
of clear white letters that fell
on my mat, only on natal days.
Now you stand in my room,
thinner than the picture memory holds,
paler than our photographs,
waiting to shed that shallow skin
for the slow soft beat of a snake-dance.

Like children, put on certain shoes,
dress in the costume of the play;
the lines of different roles we knew,
forgotten by the subtle twist of years.
Bring out a moment from the past
to make us sisters in the blood again.
In the dark alone, we are running,
skipping, dancing, never stopping,
afraid of a fairy tale. The music
doesn't change; only, we are older,
and there is a fault that underpins
the surface, bringing an earth tremor nearer,
bringing you to my door.

Kathy Miles

Moving the Boxes
(For Anabel)

This was the least I could give you:
my strength on the far side of a box
packed with your hidden life, the weight
of cheerful clutter, our years apart.
Our arms and backs were strong
together, making a dance of it.

I pushed the sides shut, and you taped
all joins and edges tight against time
and weather; our eyes met over the stacks,
we laughed a lot. You folded summer clothes
for a distant season. It was work, tough
labour, pressing the grief right down.

It was the last I could give you:
a catkin-branch from the river, a clutch
of snowdrops, their white winged faces;
my scrubbing-out of cupboards, scratch
meals from the ends of packets, a spread
of coloured cards, chances, changes.

And for me, the gathering-up of love
giving me heart again. We could see
each other now quite clearly without our men:
our perfect, matched movements, our double power.
It was no trouble. The boxes are well filled;
now for the hard part. We'll share the load.

Hilary Llewellyn-Williams

ON REACHING 40

On Becoming Forty: A Crisis of Confidence

it has taken years of careful neglect
to get this far
you don't think the garden looks like this by chance?
long grass and buttercups
cultivated carelessly
through whole summers
of forgetfulness
'like a meadow' I say with confidence

you don't think the house got this way
by chance?
all those carelessly draped shawls
the jungle of plants
the carefully hung cobwebs
the picturesque leak in the roof
no
it has taken years of careful neglect
to achieve all this
'the country look' I say with confidence

you don't think my daughter grew this way
by luck?
all those carefully planned non-sexist toddler groups
those creative flexible rules
laid down by a harrassed mum
all those survival skills she learned
as a latch-key kid
all that insight into teenage culture
no
it has taken years of careful neglect
for her to grow this way
'go eat your heart out Dr Spock', I cry with confidence

don't think I am this way
by luck or chance
it has taken years of unplanned misadventure
to get this far
a passionate improvident romance
a love child
years of unexpected single parenthood
a whole career in hustling, hobbling, penny-pinching
a thousand daily dramas met head on
a hundred cracks and bumps
a dozen crises in which I crashed and thrashed about
until accidentally
I tumbled into middle age
celebrating forty wayward years –
with confidence

Penny Windsor

A fertility goddess of the Hittite period

Slowly I let drop my slip
Undid my bra
Discarded tights
Turned deliberately
To the mirror –
Of all the sights
I resembled most
A fertility goddess of the Hittite period.

I gasped and stared crestfallen
How could the ravage of years be so cruel?
Hugging my nightie to my ample bosom
I lit a cigarette, for my thoughts, fuel.

Muriel McCarthy

The Bloody Telephone

The bloody telephone does not ring.
Visitors none – just children, charities,
And double glazing.
Grow old gracefully they say
When all within me is blazing –
Do they realize the lost years?
Supporting children alone,
Drying my tears,
Then years of illness confirm my fears –
What way out for an ageing belle:
Propanalol and the way to hell?

You have not lived yet the priest had said
Let these Americans adopt your children
Listen, start afresh.
I could not, now he is dead.
So I trundled on with a daughter and son,
Satisfaction of a good job done
There is none.

A kindly seer in an upstairs flat
Asks when you look in the mirror
What do you see?
I cringe and answer the same old me –
There is beauty in your face she says
You are attractive and have the gift
Of bringing solace to souls adrift.

Have faith, she says, all will clear,
Your time of happiness is very near
But have I not heard these words before?
The bloody telephone does not ring.
Visitors none – just children, charities,
And double glazing.

Muriel McCarthy

Thinking about Harry

She sits facing the window where wintering
gulls weave in and out of the dark
and level branches of a cedar. 'They say
my tree is more than a hundred years
old. It isn't mine of course.'
Her face is carved in a smile. Behind her
back, a blank distempered wall
separates the women's lounge from where
the old men sit and doze, or watch
snatches of Play School on the box.

Her face retains the smile. Her voice
is hoarse from lack of practice. 'There never
was anyone like Harry. I can't
see him any more, not like
I used to, in my mind. Sometimes
he's there, but I can't quite . . . ' Her grip
loosens on the wooden arms
of the chair. 'I hope . . . so long ago . . .
that when I see him I shall know

which one is Harry.' Her eyes scan
the walls, the armchairs each with its own
reclining figure. There is no picture, −
sepia fading to monochrome:
perhaps on another wall, another
room, where someone else's Harry
shifts his gaze from the toe of his shoe
to the face of a stranger smiling out
of a screen, showing him how to trace
an approximation of a face.

Eleanor Cooke

WHAT'S THE TIME

What's the time?

What's the time?

At the first strike
The time sponsored by Accurist will be
Time to wash the grass
Before the sheep can eat it
And it gets around the class

What's the time?

At the second strike
The time sponsored by Accurist will be
Time to hose the sky
That cool dome of blue
Where peace doves used to fly

What's the time?

At the third strike
From Accurist
It will be time to give the clouds a sweep
The dust gets in the eyes
And makes the whole world weep

What's the time?

At the fourth strike
From Accurist
Rainbows are fading out
The ends are dripping into streams
And poisoning the trout.

What's the time?

At the fifth strike
From Accurist
It will be time to wash the rain
You wash it and you wash it
And you rinse it down again
And you wash it and you wash it –
You can't be really sure they say
Until you've rinsed it and rinsed it
And you've rinsed the wash away.

What's the time?

I've asked the time
From Accurist
And this is what he said
'I can't tell you what the time is
I've suddenly gone dead.'

Betty Lane

Neighbours

That spring was late. We watched the sky
and studied charts for shouldering isobars.
Birds were late to pair. Crows drank from the lamb's eye.

Over Finland small birds fell: song thrushes
steering north, smudged signatures on light,
migrating warblers, nightingales.

Wing-beats failed over fjords, each lung a sip of gall.
Children were warned of their dangerous beauty.
Milk was spilt in Poland. Each quarrel

the blowback from some old story,
a mouthful of bitter air from the Ukraine
brought by the wind out of its box of sorrows.

This spring, a lamb sips caesium on a Welsh hill.
A child, lifting her face to drink the rain,
takes into her blood the poisoned arrow.

Now we are all neighbourly, each little town
in Europe twinned to Chernobyl, each heart
with the burnt fireman, the child on the Moscow train.

In the democracy of the virus and the toxin
we wait. We watch for spring migrations,
one bird returning with green in its voice.

Glasnost.
Golau glas.
A first break of blue.

Gillian Clarke

golau:light
glas:blue

The Right to Protest

A child in clown's outfit dances, smiles,
asks: 'Daddy, will I be on T.V.?'
The cameras film, she spins around,
turns a cartwheel, laughs charmingly.
The procession snakes into conference halls
listens, claps, cheers,
makes resolutions for the future.

On the next day's local news
there's no mention of the
bright-bannered demonstration,
yet camera crews took rolls of film.

Somewhere, in secret bunkers
faces and names are linked subversively;
a child in clown's costume dances into computer files.

Sue Moules

Out of the shadows . . .

The journey is taking
longer than I expected.
Nothing is as I remember it.
Last night I spent two hours
clearing a way through broken masonry.
Without the hitch-hiker's help
I couldn't have managed it.
In the rubble I picked up
part of a weathercock
– the head – and hid it from her.
(Black, not gold.)
It is for you.
I heard on the radio
personal possession is declared
delinquent. If I am
stopped and searched
before I get home, I'll have to
hand it over to the guards.
The constant cold and dark
is getting me down. It is
only the heat of our bodies
that makes sleep possible.

We wake to a grey hunger.
We collected food at a depot
three nights ago,
but now it's all gone.
I am afraid of losing my bearings.
At corners the headlights
swing into emptiness.
The driving mirror
cracked when I hit a bank; now I look up and see the road behind
brittled like a dark star.
In the passenger seat,
the hitch-hiker's profile etches
the terrible fear
that I'll never find you,
see your face again.

Eleanor Cooke

Teifi Pools

(for John and Hazel who took us there when acid rain was beginning to be recognised as a problem in Dyfed)

In the hollow of the hills'
Unfoldings where clear water seeps and gathers
The small lakes shine like scattered silver
In the white sun of mornings

But can tremble like petals.
Blue-hazy as the eyes of children
Beckoned into daydream
They blink slowly as the clouds move over.

Now at evening I see them
Streaked with slow red, as if signalling
A deep-down hurt
That can no longer be contained.

Stolid, the black horizons
Close in round them, blot them out
Except in memory, where they go on glittering
Like touchstones, bleeding.

Christine Evans

DINAS

On the Periphery

Here, now the strike
Is already fading,
But then was it ever
Anything more than a
News item, placed between
The lowering pound and the
Rising crime rate;
Days off school;
People in silly costumes
Jangling tins in the pub?

We were lucky,
The only bitterness
We felt, perhaps,
Was one of irony;
Now the only thing
They dig up is
The past
And even that is recent.

Yet we all saw the
Pictures,
Bloody photos
In black and white,
Heard cries
On the local radio
For justice.
We all condemned –
Striker, strikebreakers, leaders
Blue or red
Dancing on the sidelines.

Yes, it was all so simple
Over a pint, gin and tonic,
Coffee – cappucino or expresso,
For us who have crept from valley to vale.
For them,
Man or land,
Judas takes many forms.

Sarah Francis

Dinas Caerdydd
(An extract)

Losing your heart to the city
as dusk caresses the sky to pink
and the turrets of the Castle pirouette
against the slinking darkness –
slack-time and the night encircling
continually
ominous news reports and Echoes on the
streets again – a city's ebony descending
and getting into the rhythms of the night.
Style on the streets and the facades of the
face – erected,
a scarf knotted at the throat
with slicked-up hair
the empty gestures that
leave no trace, no mark,
of generosity –
only 'dare' beneath the mask –
pulling at the emptiness
while all over town – private assignations
at this, 'the violet hour' –
amber neon softening the blows of night
like a velvet glove.

Heartbreaker –
sex loose on the streets again
and on the Bay the
white banana boats, like ghosts,
riding the emptiness and pulling at
the vacant places in the heart with
the swoop and pull of seagulls –
skimming dark water.

The city seduced by those who wanted it
here – where they took a sledge hammer
to its heart
destroyed her streets
disturbed her communities
laid waste her green spaces and
laughed at her integrity in
the shiny sixties –
weakened the kernel with greed,
plastic and the new constructions,
but the ambiance remained
the soul intact
reality unfinished not fixed
in this city that dreamed it was
New York the immigrants flooding through
the Dockland with the flavour of Europe
running through its arteries like
the coal where
the Ironmasters ruled a man-made history –
but the past is a forbidden place,
blacker than midnight,
the dream rewinding.

Victorian city
stripped by technocrats
her panorama interfered with
her imagery undermined
the skyline battle-scarred
against the atrocity of her broken sunsets
the rhythms beneath jangling
I walked here –
Dinas Caerdydd.

What could be more absurd
than the weight of the past
with this thin veil of realism?
Reality is not fixed –
it translates the sense of
place, of hiraeth or of home
and the skein is lifted, but
where does the balance fall?

The onslaught
the cacophony of sounds
the traffic overhead
the sky pass where
bikers flirt with suicide
the sky an unreal blue
beneath the sprawling city
streets littered like an alien
civilisation the hovering aircraft
the television masts far out
the menace of an underground shelter
plans for catastrophe kept secret
rain falling mud in the river
the distant hills
and the light the light
for ever changing –
spring almost in the city
felt on the air in this chaos of
activity as the future waits.

> And at the Cha Cha Video Cafe
> you turn your collar up –
> as in an old movie
> Facade, Lady.

The taproot – the street life
the man who plays piano
beneath a green umbrella
a woman fingering a saxaphone,
the buskers and the violin players,
the poets in pubs – leaning on bars waiting
to die 'in camera' – an instant legend.
Purveyors of delight – traders in the fantastic
punks, pushers, police and vagrants
with great subtlety serenade this city
while idle tea-drinkers search for a
lost elegance as the world goes by
and pigeons settle on flagstones
content with crumbs
the cry of street vendors and in the
tulip gardens the graves lying
quietly by.

Gill Brightmore

A Saturday in the '20s

The child came to the dark library,
Afraid. Feeling the darkness of the men
Sitting so silently – not reading –
On the tilted chairs.

The steps to go in were loaded with darkness.
Men stood hinged on their heavy arms.
A smell of cloth pudding boiling on a winter day –
The child knew this smell.
Damp caps over embittered minds, they smell the same.
Men's gear stricken; like the ancient smoke
Above the table. No one was smoking
Yet there it hung.

Then the lame man sumped with his keys,
Opening cases,
Muttering. What was a child doing here,
Among darkened men? Wanting locked books?
The child snatched and fled

While the books bloomed in a fire between covers,
Waiting to burst for her – Saturday's great new rose.
The men lolled silent, holding their empty hands
On their dark knees. She was afraid.
Yet beyond fear, she wanted their books
That they did not read.

What the dark men wanted
She was too young and well-cared for
To understand.

Jean Earle

Heron at Port Talbot

Snow falls on the cooling towers
delicately settling on cranes.
Machinery's old bones whiten; death
settles with its rusts, its erosions.

Warning of winds off the sea
the motorway dips to the dock's edge.
My hands tighten on the wheel against
the white steel of the wind.

Then we almost touch, both braking flight,
bank on the air and feel that shocking
intimacy of near-collision,
animal tracks that cross in snow.

I see his living eye, his change of mind,
feel pressure as we bank, the force
of his beauty. We might have died
in some terrible conjunction.

The steel town's sulphurs billow
like dirty washing. The sky stains
with steely inks and fires, chemical
rustings, salt-grains, sand under snow.

And the bird comes, a surveyor
calculating space between old workings
and the mountain hinterland, archangel
come to re-open the heron-roads,

meets me at an inter-section
where wind comes flashing off water
interrupting the warp of snow
and the broken rhythms of blood.

Gillian Clarke

Sheep on the Brecon hills

Salmon
     Swim over ancient cobbles,
Mirror dancing through mirror,
               Sheep
On the Brecon hills
   Framed between chimney pots
Of the town,
     Each fragrance
With the smell of cut grass;
       In holiday jobs
Teenage schoolgirls
   Abhor wearing National costume.

The Market clock
       Stopped for over a century
   Displays
An Out of Order notice
 For the tourists,
     Roses around the door
Of a firm of solicitors,
         A butterfly
With quarrelling wings.

        On half-drowned banks
Of a carpeted pool
   Picnickers
     Beneath a birch
As if silvered
     Only by the wind.

Gloria Evans Davies

June Exercise

Unzipping
smooth blue silence
four low-flying Phantoms
squeal up from the south
and hurtle towards Aberdaron

hawk shadows
making the sun blink
as if it too were blotted out by noise,
light wincing
on sprawled bodies in the sand.

The woman at the water's edge
with a naked baby on her hip
and one arm raised to shield her eyes
is a speck they lock onto at six o'clock:

obliterated in a tide of flame
that surges further
than the sea has ever done
and drowns the village

as the jets peel off, rising swiftly
slitting the sky towards Ireland
at a thousand miles an hour
and wave after wave of booming
slackens, rumbles, slides into a purr.

Nothing cowers before them:
a few sheep still scatter and seabirds
screaming, fling themselves off
to float up and blow away
like ashes. The nest-sites
ring, but on the beaches
no more than a half-dozen bodies
have been stirred, turned over
to get the other side done.

Christine Evans

JOURNEY TO BETHLEHEM

Journey to Bethlehem

We dined at Bethlehem,
Orange Free State,
While travelling to witness
Swaziland's Independence Day.
A dark drive through high veldt
To the Afrikaans laager of light.

Burdened by our values,
Shackled by liberalism
We trudged to the dorp's hotel.
In its barn of a dining-room, three
White-gloved, red-fezzed black men
Served us solemnly as kings.

In that segregated silence
Nothing was holy.
We gave no gifts,
But, over-tipped.
Refreshed, we resumed our trek,
To someone else's independence.

Gillian Fothergill

The Villages

You pass through my village, people behind glass. My wise cow ignores
     you.
See how he grazes on straw and paper in the concrete yard.
This water I carry for him.
This dust is our gold, is the earth my mother stoops to turn in the field,
Is the dung my sister works into cakes, is the walls of my house.
In the city you will see my father.
He lives in a house with neither walls nor roof.
Tell him – my cow is so wise he will always come home at night.
One day, in plastic shoes, I will travel myself and tell him.
When you have gone, aeroplane people, I and my cow, with these roving
animals, will trample out your tracks.
Our dust you may take with you. You will leave nothing here.

Madeline Mayne

Victory for Mandela

Blood on the walls
Screams from a cellar
Bars on the doors
Shadow behind the bars
The shadow of a man
            White in the dark of the night
            Black in the light.

This man is a mother's son
This man has arms like a lover
This man can father a child
This man is a brother
            White in the dark of the night
            Black in the light.

He longs for the sun on his face and the rain
He longs to walk in the woods and swim in the sea
He longs to breathe fresh air, be with his family.
He has been offered a twisted key –
'If you do what we tell you, you're free'
            White in the dark of the night
            Black in the light.

He can if he wished to walk free, –
But only by using this twisted key
That lets his body through the door
And leaves his mind and his soul behind.
His will is his own in his cell
His cell, his territory. So he stays
        Locked in, to victory.
        Locked in, to victory.

Blood on the walls
Screams from a cellar
Bars on the doors
Shadow behind the bars
The shadow of a man
        White in the dark of the night
        Black in the light.

Betty Lane

Varanasi

We are too poor to need anything.
We stand and look at you, aeroplane people, people in the coach,
Asking for nothing.
From the dust between our toes, from the straw of our houses,
We will spin you a golden thread,
From mulberry silk weave your cloth of gold to throw around
    your shoulders.
We will see you at dawn, with the tossed marigolds,
Bulbuls, temple bells, umbels, by the brown burning Ganges,
Where the sun sets light to the Ghats.
Aeroplane people, go away from us as flames go, as dreams go.
Leave us, who are too poor to ask anything of you.

Madeline Mayne

LAST RITES

Last Rites

During this summer of the long drought
The road to Synod Inn has kept
Its stigmata of dust and barley seed;

At the inquest they tell it again:
How the lorry tents us from the sun,
His pulse dangerous in my hands,
A mains hum only, no message
Coming through. His face warm, profiled
Against tarmac, the two-stroke Yamaha
Dead as a black horse in a war.
Only his hair moves and the sound
Of the parched grass and harebells a handspan
Away, his fear still with me like the scream
Of a jet in an empty sky.
I cover him with the grey blanket
From my bed, touch his face as a child
Who makes her favourites cosy.
His blood on my hands, his cariad in my arms.

Driving her home we share that vision
Over August fields dying of drought
Of the summer seas shattering
At every turn of Cardigan Bay
Under the cruel stones of the sun.

Gillian Clarke

Granny T's Revenge
(born, lived and died Pendeen, Cornwall)

She had scant regard for men
'like bulls' she used to say
arms akimbo
'pick out the prizes for breeding
and shoot the rest.'

One of eighteen
father long gone abroad
never returned
mother dead from overwork
she, fifteen or so,
brought up the rest.
She had scant regard for men.

Later, she married Grandpa T. –
Spanish looking with a fine moustache.
They had two sons and four daughters
when he left for America –
to find gold, he said.

The boys were sent down Geevor Mine
an afterthought.
The girls she educated
to be independent, fierce
with scant regard for men.
They married foreigners
from Bristol, Somerset
and came to live near Granny T,
sharing family life and the family grave.

She died a few years back
still angry, blind
with scant regard for men
and left a will –
'I wish', she wrote
'to be buried in the family grave
on top of Grandpa T.'

She had scant regard for men
but this time
there was to be no getting away.

Penny Windsor

He lived

He lived in an empty name in a foreign land.
The barrier broken momentarily when he asked
Yet again
The English for 'scissors'.
I was sometimes Gillian, sometimes me.
He never said what he never did
And he was never ill if he didn't want to be
Well, not to me.
'You don't want this rubbish', he would say
In a shop and I would turn red,
And sigh, perhaps I didn't.
He would buy us everything
And the cloth to wrap it in.
A good tailored fit described in detail
The London office, the Vienna roots,
The peppermint.
It was ironic in the end.
For he had travelled all his life.

Kate Cumming

The Bronchoscopy Session 1969

You are on the table.
This was a room once, but its bay window is
Now shuttered. There is
Non-specific space in the bay. There is
A fireplace tiled over with brown tiles,
A warmth of colour from cold glaze.
There is
Quietness.

You are on the table.
You have had a throatful of local anaesthetic,
Purple,
Bitter.

We take our accustomed places. There is
A syringe on your arm, the needle in place,
Nine millilitres of acquiescence. There is
A rigid metal tube. There is
Quietness.

You are on the table.
You have had two millilitres of acquiescence.
Your eyes are covered by a green cloth.
Your neck, your pliant neck, is extended.
You grip my hand.

We start our accustomed procedure. There is
A green light, a cold light, in the tube. There is
A moment of manoeuvering. There is
A cough, a rush of air through the bronchoscope.
Glasses misted up in exhaled dampness.
Two more millilitres of acquiescence. There is
Quietness.

You are on the table.
We do not accuse.
We do not condemn,
We do not execute.
If sentence is passed we will get you what reprieve we can.

You are on the table.
Your head is positioned and repositioned.
This is what you will remember,
This obedience,
This loss of your own volition.

The examination is being made. There is
A knife edge where the bronchi diverge. There is
A ridged hollow tube, red, mobile. There is
An abnormality, an occlusion. There is
A rampant cancer. There is
Quietness.

You are on the table.
You are a clerk.
You have children, your delight.
You have a world with its own contours, your individual perception.

The examination is being made. There is
A snake mouthed instrument. There is
A moment's manipulation. There is
A fragment of tissue in formalin. There is
Quietness.

You are on the table.
You are a mother but you have always hated living.
How will you hate dying?

The examination is being made.
The bronchus is being irrigated for malignant cells. There is
A command to cough, a rigid whip sucker. There is
A hissing sibilance. There is
Quietness.

You are on the table.
You are a shepherd.
You have toted bales of hay to the winter hillside.
You have sheared grey tattered warm sheep.
You have been a strength.
You have known the companionships of living.

You are on the table.
We do not accuse.
We do not condemn.
We do not execute.
The sentence is passed. We will get you what reprieve we can.
It is something you knew but had not thought of in this context.

The examination has been made.
The bronchoscope has been withdrawn. There is
Relaxation. There is
The task of recording. There is
Quietness.

You are on the table.
Your eyes are uncovered.
You look around.
You want to know what we cannot tell you.
You are told 'There are some results to wait for.
An examination is being made.'

Madeline Mayne

Conversation 1

'It seems to take a long time,
dying.' Her eyes rested on
the flowers I'd brought, late buds
of roses stopped by a chancy frost.
'I have been wondering how best
to look, what position to be
in, when I die.' Her hand
lifted and fell. 'I have been
practising, lying here,' – and still
she lay just as she had the last
time they came to turn her. 'I
suppose it's funny,' and she smiled,
and slept. I sat, picking at
a rose, teasing the tight bud open.
Under her closed eyelids her limbs
were gracefully disposed; angle of
head, a sideways tilt, hands
and fingers loosely curved – a plaster
hand on a gaming table – the gentle
coquetrie of chin and cheek,
the late bloom of a smile.

Eleanor Cooke

10.40 p.m. 27th February

This morning I walked the shining corridors in a dream
You were there still, ward 2, third on the right
I looked at you, measuring your life
I've always known that you must die
But hoped it wouldn't be today
You sat in bed, leaning to one side
Jaw loose, skin pale, eyes paler still
Half seeing me, mistier than the winter sky
I've always feared that you would die
But hoped it wouldn't be today
Old women sat in chairs beside their beds, each solitary
Or shuffled by, practising ghosts
They looked more frail than you
Such ancient scales I measured by
I've always known that you would die
But hoped it wouldn't be today.

This evening your empty bed is neat
Old women sit in chairs, each solitary
Or shuffle by; they look so well
I've always known that you must die
But hoped it wouldn't be today
They hand me the clothes, rings, certificate,
I thank them for their care,
We say goodbye
I've always feared that you would die
But hoped it wouldn't be today.

I'll be pleased to have the piano
I learned to play on it when I was eight
But what shall I do with the clothes
Take them to Oxfam, someone will be glad of them
I've always known that you would die
But hoped it wouldn't be today.
You walk alone on a vast plain
Moving away, moving away, moving away,
From the dark hole, the smoking sky.

Betty Lane

MISSA

Missa Pontcanna

Forty years confined
in the sisterhood of silence. Noise to her
was chink of rosary, footfall
on gravel in a walled garden,
trapped song of blackbird
the hour before Angelus.

In a world unimagined before today
she shared the night with a crowd gathering
in darkness like a great migration,
the dawn moon dissolving,
the rose-window of the rising sun.

She has known in one dazzling day
circus and sea-side, fair-day and birthday,
oratorio, picnic, holy day, holiday,
crowd, Kyrie, caritas, caru,
and a Pope behind glass, his smile distant
after television's intimacy.

First sight of the world –
a hundred thousand picnic by a river,
the old faint in the heat, the young
sunbathe profanely, diving for joy in the Taff.
First sound after silence a crowd's roar
under yellow flags like barley in the wind.

Catching her patience the Taff loiters
in shadows, falls in a wimple of pleats
over Blackweir counting its prayer on stones.
Dizzy, sunburnt, as at the close of any
secular day, they queue for the bridge.
Thunder growls and the rain begins.

Something is over. In the cell of herself
the day stores its honey and an image
of the world for whose salvation
she tells and tells her beads.

Gillian Clarke

Householder

He is one of my landmarks
the old man I see each morning
in his shirtsleeves, testing the air
outside his front door, braced and gaunt
against an east wind or mindless of rain
face lifted keenly like a muzzle
to the light. In summer I have seen him
leaning on the gate and looking out
with something of a sailor's hunger
to see beyond the white-thorned banks.
If he is turned to go in
I know I am late.

When there is sun, it is behind him.
I do not look for recognition
more than from a badger
reconnoitring. I shall not know his name
or what language he is thinking in
but some morning soon
there will be strangers' cars outside
and only a shadow like a tree across the road
to tell me how the time is going.

Christine Evans

Breadmaking

Forgive the flour under my fingernails
the dabs of dough clinging to my skin:
I have been busy, breadmaking.
So easy, the flakes falling feathery
into the warm bowl, as I dip and measure
and pour the foaming treasured brown
yeast down to the ground wheat grain.
O as the barm breaks and scatters
under my working fingers like a scum
of tides on shifting sands, the secret cells
swell, you can smell their life
feeding and beating like blood
in my bunched palms
while I lift the lump and slap it back again.

It moves, like a morning mushroom,
a breathing side, stirring, uncurling
animal nudged from sleep; so I pummel
and thump and knuckle it into shape
to see it unwind like a spring
soft as a boneless baby on the table.
I have covered it now: let it grow
quietly, save for the least rustle
of multiplication in the damp bundle
telling of motion in the fattening seeds.
Its body's an uproar as I open the burning door –
it gives one final heave, and it blossoms out
to the brown loaf I have spread for you.
Taste the butter touching its heart like snow.

Hilary Llewellyn-Williams

Father goes blackberrying

He rakes the hedges for blackberries.
His hands, cool as snowballs,
ignore the thorns
that tease the slow blood.
He looks at his fingers, thumb,
sees the skin purple with juice.
Tired, he glances at the horizon,
blinking away
the printed tangle of hawthorn,
old man's beard, and sun-black fruit
that lingers in his eyes.
He looks this way and that.
The lane mirrors itself.
Confused, he takes a few steps,
turns,
retraces them,
and knows that he is lost.
He feels a solitary drop of rain
on his cheek,
looks up into a cloudless sky.
He chances his luck, and strides out
bravely.
His shadow, walking ahead of him,
whispers in the voice of a boy,
seven, eight, nine, ...
counting each step
between the empty schoolyard
and the door
his mother has left open
to catch the evening sun.

Eleanor Cooke

The Trespasser

My fingers are sweet with stealing
blackcurrants. Among tall weeds
ropes of them, thick and ripe like secrets.
I move in shadow, sharpeyed, listening.
A distant car sets my spine quivering.
Bold as a bird I pull the berries down,
gather them in. Their smell excites me.

The house is blind: no one is living here,
yet I am trespassing. Each summer the owners
come for a week or two, cut grass,
clean windows, stare out from their gate.
But the river sings all year; and swifts make
nests, flowers bloom and fruit
ripens, and snow sweeps the lawn
smooth for the prints of foxes.

In spring there were daffodils, massed gold
and white narcissi; I ran in the rain
to gather armfuls, carrying them home
to shine in my windows. I live by here
every day, in poverty. What the hedges grow,
what's in the hills, I take back for my children.

Great polished blackcurrants in my fist.
They drop in the bag, grow fat.
Tonight I'll mix them with sugar, and steam
them slowly. The dark, sour, smokey taste;
my children's red mouths and chins,
their high, bird voices. Each year the trees
step forward round the house: I notice that.
In the autumn, I'll come for apples.

Hilary Llewellyn-Williams

Chutney Jars

Her larder contained
assorted jars of chutney.
So many colours and textures
labelled and dated.
Each displayed month, year.
She remembered events
by reading the stickers.
Recalled the sweet smell
of simmering seasons:
the clothes she wore,
her current lover.
Days of events poured
from the recollections –
kept her thinking all day,
at night she replaced the jar
to preserve her memories.

Sue Moules

CONTACT PRINT

Portrait-Gallery

The mirror follows her round
with its square eye. Sometimes
reflection is clear as water,
outlines ignored by the cold glass.
Movement is swallowed into the frame,
turned in on itself, reversed.
Figures are trapped inside her room;
forms that appear from another world
are fused into sand and silver.
Old, alone, she waits like a spider
to pounce on their polished shadows.
The door is empty of callers,
but yellow light beckons these silent
visitors, bodies are stolen from the street,
stories woven round their glazed white faces.
Here she sees the passing of the cars,
rain falling beyond the mantelpiece.
Sun is a beam that strikes the pane,
sucked down to fire's pale shining.
Walls and ceilings are repeated, like
a maze without an exit. Memory floats
in the loom of these corners, connects
in half-remembered fables. Now
she weaves her own small plans,
watches for the breaking of the glass.

Kathy Miles

Contact Print

Emphatic, a hand
Printed itself, a mud

Impact on a cave
Wall. There,
Just like that, it was

Done. Almost needing
To check, I want to

Press my palm
Against it, measuring
The differences.

Wrinkled as a map,
Lines contour hills,

Dips in grooves, returning
To themselves in loops
At fingertips. I wonder

If my hand would
Fit that mould, if

Across a breadth
Of time, a faint
Pulse could be felt;

Like scars
Unhealing, would lifelines

Join for a moment,
Run parallel, twine
In a single strand

Placed crease to crease
Hand to hand?

Frances Williams

Bushmen Cave Paintings

Undistinguished by signs:
'To Ancient Monument',
By tea shops, or by car park,
That Basotho village, like all others,
Was remarkable for children.

When we parked, the rotund black pigs
Continued their peaceable scavenging,
The village adults smiled shyly,
While from every rondavel
Children catapulted out.́

Small, blanketed, chirruping,
They respectfully laid siege,
Cupped hands, asked for sweets.
'Cave paintings?' we said;
Broke chocolate, struck a bargain.

Singing, they led us to the rocks.
Dismayed, we saw the dull,
Static, childish scrawls.
Then the children filled their cheeks
With water from the stream, and spat.

Suddenly, the little men quickened,
Speared leaping buck,
Combined to stab the crocodile,
Momentarily clasped their wives,
Until the dry air stifled them.

Silently we trudged back,
Children tired. One tiny boy
I carried, when he fell behind,
Coughing; frail as a painted matchstick man,
Too easily eclipsed.

Gillian Fothergill

Vessel

This jug has eyes, fish
Disced that watch unblinking, wide

Open through centuries. From serf
To knight, many have drunk
From it. Ears also serve
As handles, the mouth ready

To spout all liquid secrets
From a fat girth. 'Pour me',

She says 'And I will sing
My music, spill my soul,
Swill your glass with old
Spirit. My load has no

Odour, cannot be seen
In any colour. I have spent

My songs on many others
Who have been less
Sturdy in their form than I'.

Frances Williams

CONTRIBUTORS

Jude Brigley was born in Maesteg, Mid Glamorgan. She teaches English at St Ilan Comprehensive School, Caerphilly. She is a director of the poetry performance group Poetry Unlimited.

Gillian Brightmore was born in Llantrisant. She read English at University College of Swansea, followed by a Master's degree course at McMaster University, Ontario. She has worked in adult education since 1981 and currently runs a women's creative writing group at University of Wales, College of Cardiff. She is a member of the Cardiff-based women's performance group Deadlier Than The Male. She has been writing for some eight years and is at present concentrating on writing plays. 'Dinas' is part of a longer poem celebrating the city of Cardiff.

Gillian Clarke was born in Cardiff in 1937 and has lived in Dyfed since 1984. Her collections of poetry include *The Sundial* (Gwasg Gomer, 1978); *Letter From a Far Country* (1982), *Selected Poems* (1985), and *Letting in the Rumour* (1989), all from Carcanet. *Letting in the Rumour* was a Poetry Book Society recommendation and was on the poetry shortlist for the Whitbread Prize 1989.

Eleanor Cooke was born and brought up in Yorkshire. She now lives on the Cheshire/Shropshire borders. She has worked as a writer and poet in schools and colleges and with teachers' in-service training groups. Her poetry has appeared in many magazines and anthologies, and on radio, and she has a collection *A Kind of Memory* published by Seren Books. Her long poem/documentary *Who Killed Prees Heath?* was featured on a Kaleidoscope programme on BBC Radio 4, a programme which was later commended in the *Prix Italia* awards.

Kate Cumming was born in Scotland and brought up in Hereford and Caerphilly. She is a student at the College of St Mark and St John, Plymouth. She is a member of Poetry Unlimited, a performance poetry group which plays at schools, colleges, pubs etc.

Jean Earle is English but has spent most of her life in Wales. She has recently retired to Shrewsbury. During the 1930s she wrote short stories and did radio work. Following a twenty-year break she began to write poetry and has since published *Trial of Strength* (Carcanet), *The Intent Look* (Gomer), and *Visiting Light* (Poetry Wales Press). She was awarded a Welsh Arts Council Prize for *Trial of Strength* and *Visiting Light* was a Poetry Book Society Choice. Seren Books will publish a volume of new and selected poems in 1990.

Christine Evans lives on a smallholding in Llŷn. In 1982 she returned to a full-time job teaching English in Pwllheli. Born and brought up in a cotton-mill town in West Yorkshire, she remembered her grandmother speaking Welsh, which gave her pleasure in learning it – though even twenty years on, erratic tenses and unreliable endings keep her quieter than she would like! A scribbler from childhood, she did not start writing seriously, that is for an audience, until her mid thirties. She has published three books of poetry, is completing a fourth, and is trying to write short stories.

Gloria Evans Davies was born in Maesteg. She left school at the age of fourteen and has spent most of her life in Carmarthenshire and Breconshire. Her work has appeared in many magazines and anthologies. The volumes *Words for Blodwen* and *Her Name Like the Hours* were published by Chatto and Windus. She is currently preparing a third volume of poems.

Gillian Fothergill was born in Scotland. She has taught and written in Lesotho, Scotland and the Welsh Marches. She now lives in Caerphilly and teaches in Mid Glamorgan.

Sarah Francis was born in Bridgend in 1966 and has spent most of her life in south Wales. She was educated at Brynteg Comprehensive School and Girton College, Cambridge, where she read English literature. During her time at Cambridge, she was women's officer for her college and was involved in several projects to improve access and conditions for women students. She has spent a year teaching in Kenya and has travelled to a number of other African countries. Her work has appeared in *Poetry Wales*.

Betty Lane studied at Cardiff College of Art and with her husband set up a pottery in a cottage in Penzance. Single again, she returned to Cardiff to follow a degree course in social psychology. She is a part-time counsellor and lecturer and, with her partner, helps to run Bojangles, a small graphics workshop. Her collection *Passionate Landscape* was published recently.

Hilary Llewellyn-Williams was born in Kent of Welsh and Anglo-Spanish parents and spent a nomadic childhood and early adulthood before settling in west Wales in 1982. She began writing at the age of seven and by the early 1970s was having some success in small poetry magazines. For ten years she almost stopped writing but began again after moving to Wales. Her first collection *The Tree Calendar* was published in 1987 and she has recently completed a second volume.

Madeline Mayne was born in Yorkshire but now lives in Carmarthen. She worked as a physician in Wales from 1973 to 1984 when she retired on health grounds. In 1983, she won second prize in the Welsh Arts Council's New Poets Competition. Her poems have been published in Macmillan's *Young Writer's Tales 7* and in two anthologies *Sotheby's 1982 Anthology* for the Arvon Foundation and in *Poets against Apartheid*, as well as in various magazines. A novel *The Lord Sun* was published in 1986.

Kathy Miles was born in Liverpool and now lives near Lampeter, where she works as a senior library assistant at St David's University College. She has had poetry and stories published in many magazines, including *Poetry Wales*, *Planet*, *New Welsh Review* and *Outposts*. Her first collection of poems,

The Rocking Stone, was published by Poetry Wales Press in June 1988.

Sue Moules is a freelance journalist and poet. Her work has been widely published in magazines and anthologies and was recently featured in a Canadian anthology, *A Labour of Love*. Her work was commended in the Welsh Arts Council's On My Life autobiographical essay competition. In 1988 she was highly commended in the Scottish National Open Poetry Competition and won second prize in the York Open Poetry Competition in 1989.

Muriel McCarthy was born in Liverpool. She moved to mid Wales as a child and was educated there, in Paris and in south Wales. In Paris she held a variety of posts including business executive, translator to the military attaché at the Indian Embassy, ambassador's secretary Republic of Korea, senior administrative assistant European Space Agency. She taught in south Wales for seventeen years. Muriel McCarthy is a sculptress and has a Master's degree from the Royal Academy of Art.

Frances Williams was born in Bridgend in 1968 and is a student of fine art at Liverpool. Next year she will be following an MA course in sculpture at Chelsea College of Art. In 1986 she won the Young Writers' Competition at the Cardiff Literature Festival, and in 1987 her volume *Flotsam* was published by Poetry Wales Press. Her latest volume *Cometary Phases* was published by Seren Books in 1989.

Penny Windsor was born in 1946 and brought up in the West Country but has lived in Swansea for the past twenty years. She has held a wide variety of jobs, in recent years working mainly as a teacher and youth worker. She is now a full-time writer. Her poems have been published in numerous periodicals, including *Spare Rib*, *Poetry Wales* and *Stand*. Her most recent collections *Dangerous Women* (1987) and *Like Oranges* (1989) were both published by Honno. Penny Windsor is well known as a performance poet.